W9-ARG-916

LEMURS

Lorien Kite

Grolier
an imprint of

www.scholastic.com/librarypublishing

Published 2009 by Grolier
An Imprint of Scholastic Library Publishing
Old Sherman Turnpike
Danbury, Connecticut 06816

For The Brown Reference Group
Project Editor: Jolyon Goddard
Picture Researchers: Clare Newman, Sophie
Mortimer
Designer: Sarah Williams
Managing Editor: Tim Harris

Volume ISBN-13: 978-0-7172-8070-4
Volume ISBN-10: 0-7172-8070-5

**Library of Congress
Cataloging-in-Publication Data**

Nature's children. Set 6.
    p. cm.
  Includes index.
  ISBN-13: 978-0-7172-8085-8
  ISBN-10: 0-7172-8085-3
  1. Animals--Encyclopedias, Juvenile. I.
Grolier (Firm)
  QL49.N387 2009
  590.3--dc22
                        2008014675

Printed and bound in China

PICTURE CREDITS

Front Cover: **Shutterstock**: Christian
Riedel.

Back Cover: **Shutterstock**: Ziv Bar,
Mariuspopma, Simone van den Berg,
Ronald van der Beek.

Corbis: ABPL 33, Wolfgang Kaehler 38;
Fotolia: Michael Luckett 5; **NHPA**: Agence
Nature 22, Nigel J. Dennis 6, 21, 25, 30, 46,
Martin Harvey 9, 10, 13, 14, 17, 18, 29, 36–37,
42, Daniel Hueclin 45; **Shutterstock**: Henk
Bentlage 4, Dariush M. 26, Petr Masek 2–3,
Christian Riedel 41.

Contents

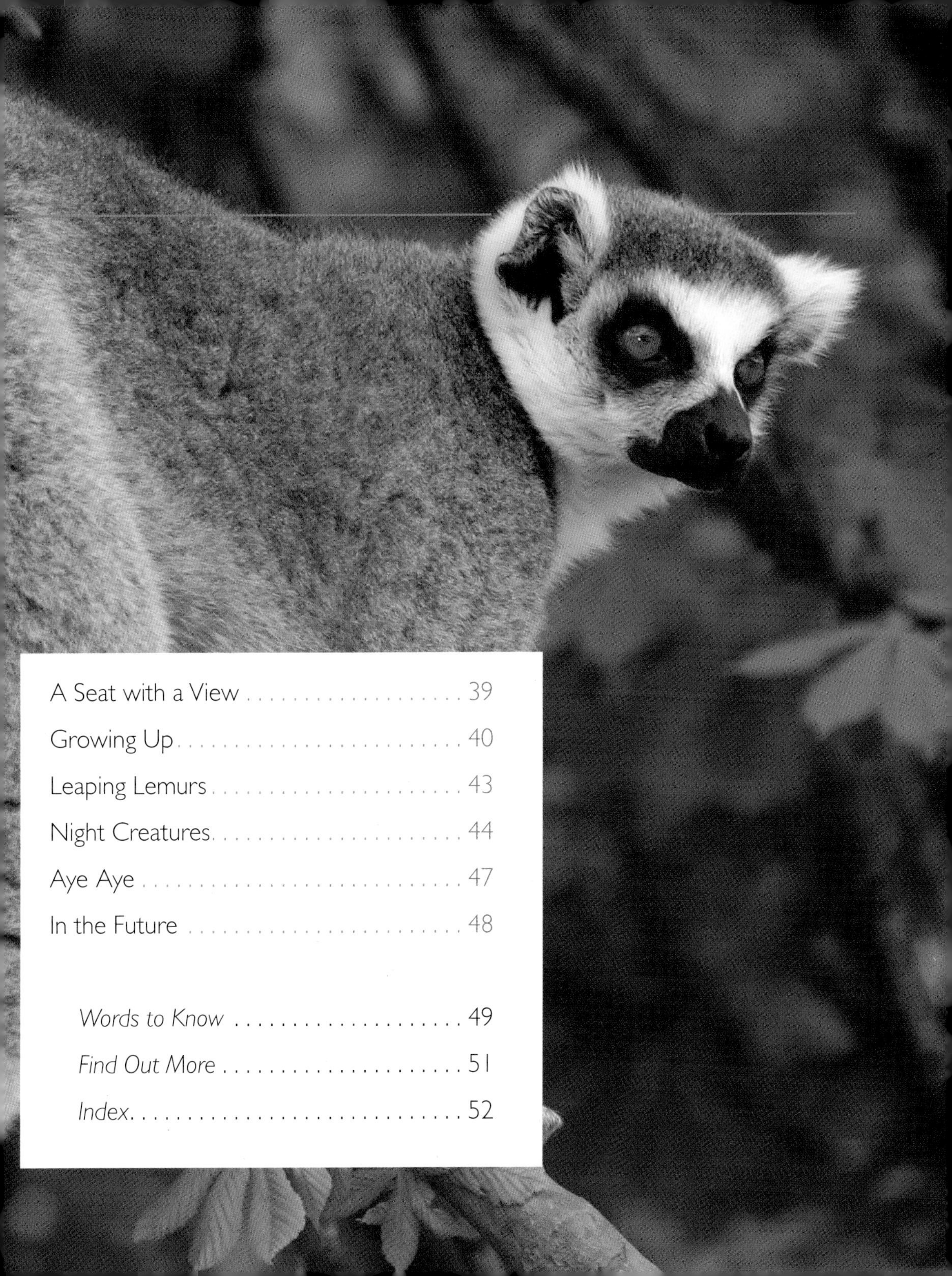

FACT FILE: Lemurs

Class	Mammals (Mammalia)
Order	Lemurs, tarsiers, monkeys, and apes (Primates)
Families	Five families
Genera	15 genera
Species	62 species
World distribution	Madagascar
Habitat	Tropical rain forests, dry woodlands, and desert scrublands
Distinctive physical characteristics	Forward-pointing eyes; a pointed snout, with a moist nose; legs longer than arms; long fingers tipped with nails; opposable thumbs; almost all species have a long, bushy tail
Habits	Most species are very sociable and live in groups of up to 30 animals; groups are territorial; mothers carry their young on their back
Diet	Fruit, leaves, buds, bark, flowers, and insects

Introduction

The word *lemur* comes from the Latin words for "spirits of the dead" or "ghosts." Perhaps that is because lemurs have odd staring eyes and some have a wailing cry. However, lemurs are not at all scary! They are fascinating animals. Lemurs have amazing climbing skills and can leap great distances. Female lemurs make excellent mothers. Many types of lemurs live in groups that are ruled by the female members!

Like other mammals, lemurs feed and care for their young.

Long, flexible fingers allow lemurs to hold onto thin branches.

A Cat with Hands?

To which group of animals do the lemurs belong? They have a doglike face, with a pointed snout and a damp, black nose. However, if you were to see one leaping from branch to branch or walking along on the forest floor, tail high in the air, you could easily mistake it for a member of the cat family.

If you need a clue, look closely at a lemur's hands. A lemur's hands are similar to a human's! Their long fingers have nails rather than claws, and just like a person, they have an **opposable thumb** on each hand. That means that they can press their thumb against the fingers of the same hand. Having an opposable thumb allows lemurs to pick things up and hold onto branches when they climb. So, which group of animals do lemurs belong to? The **primates**!

Family Business

Lemurs belong to a group of animals called primates. Monkeys, apes, and humans are also primates. Monkeys and apes are known as higher primates, or **simians**. Lemurs, on the other hand, are **prosimians**, which means "forerunners of the monkeys and apes." Like monkeys and apes, lemurs are good climbers and like to live in groups. They are smart, too, but not as smart as the simians. They cannot use tools, and they are not very good at solving problems.

Another way in which lemurs are different from monkeys and apes is that lemurs have a far more powerful sense of smell. While monkeys and apes rely mainly on sight and hearing, lemurs can sniff out ripe fruit from great distances. They often use scent to communicate with one another, too.

A ring-tailed lemur uses its moist, doglike nose to sniff out food.

A ring-tailed lemur enjoys the peace of its monkey-free home in Madagascar.

Smart Cousins

Lemurs are found only in Madagascar, a large island in the Indian Ocean 185 miles (300 km) off the eastern coast of Africa. At one time, there were lemurs living all over the world. However, when monkeys arrived on the scene, about 30 million years ago, the numbers of lemurs started to decline.

Lemurs were unable to compete with the monkeys. The new group of animals was smarter, stronger, and ate the same kinds of foods. As a result, all the lemurs living alongside the monkeys died out. The only prosimians living on mainland Africa, Asia, and the Americas today are small, timid creatures that come out only at night, when monkeys are asleep.

In Madagascar, lemurs not only survived— they flourished. When they reached the island, millions of years ago, it was very close to mainland Africa. By the time the monkeys appeared in Africa, Madagascar had drifted too far for monkeys to make the crossing.

An Island Home

Madagascar is a huge island, nearly 1,000 miles
(1,600 km) long and 360 miles (580 km) broad
at its widest point. A large mountain range runs
from north to south, splitting the island in two.
The climate is warm but differs greatly on either
side of the mountains. The land to the east is
drenched with rain all year round, whereas
in the west there is a long dry season. In the
extreme southwest of the island, **droughts**
can last for as long as 18 months.

Lemurs can be found all over Madagascar.
There are 62 **species** living in **habitats** ranging
from moist, tropical **rain forest** to **spiny desert**.
A spiny desert is an arid grassland, scattered
with large, cactuslike trees. Lemurs are absent
only in the central highlands, where most of the
trees have been chopped down.

Crossing with care—these crowned lemurs must climb over high, razor-sharp rocks to get from one forest area to another.

With its teddy bear ears and large, round eyes the indri is a memorable sight.

Little and Large

Lemurs come in many shapes and sizes. The indri is the largest species at about 2½ feet (70 cm) tall. The mouse lemur is the smallest. It grows up to 9½ inches (24 cm) from head to tail.

As Madagascar is difficult to get to, many common African animal species have never reached the island. Therefore, on Madagascar, some species of lemurs have specially **adapted** themselves. These adaptations allow the lemurs to take advantage of foods that would otherwise be eaten by other animals—if they had made it to the island. For example, the aye aye lives on grubs and wood-boring beetles, just like a woodpecker. It has very sharp teeth for biting through bark and a long, spindly third finger that it uses to pick out grubs and insects.

The best-known and most widespread lemur is the ring-tailed lemur. It is about the size of a domestic cat, but it has a huge tail. Most ring-tailed lemurs live in forests, although they can also survive in dry areas such as the spiny desert.

Getting Around

Ring-tailed lemurs spend most of their time clambering around in the treetops. Their huge tail works like a trapeze artist's pole, allowing them to balance with ease on thin branches.

Opposable thumbs on both their hands and their feet make lemurs excellent climbers. The soles of their feet are covered with tough, gripping pads that stop them from slipping. Their back legs are very strong and slightly longer than their arms. If necessary, lemurs can make great leaps from branch to branch.

Although ring-tailed lemurs spend much of their time in the treetops, where most of their food is, they are also perfectly at home on the forest floor. They walk on all fours with their rear end slightly raised and their tail held high in the air.

Two ring-tailed lemurs search for food. Their nonslip feet are extremely useful as they climb higher and higher.

A sifaka lemur makes a carefully judged leap high in the branches.

Double Vision

Most birds, fish, and small mammals have eyes that point in opposite directions. That gives them all-round vision, so they are rarely caught by surprise.

There is one disadvantage to this design—it is easier to tell how far away things are by comparing the view from one eye with that of the other. Animals whose eyes point in opposite directions cannot compare views in this way, because the views from each eye do not overlap.

The ability to judge distances is extremely important for animals that leap from branch to branch in the forest—even the tiniest mistake could lead to a fatal fall. That is why lemurs, along with monkeys and apes, have forward-facing eyes.

On the Menu

Ring-tailed lemurs are anything but fussy eaters. Their favorite food is fruit, but when that is scarce, they will happily eat young, tender leaves, bark, flowers, and insects.

Ring-tailed lemurs can bite through tough fruits with their sharp front teeth, but they prefer to eat soft, juicy fruits such as figs and bananas. They chew the soft flesh of the fruit thoroughly before swallowing. To avoid dripping sticky fruit juice on their fur, they hold their head up in the air as they eat.

Like all primates, lemurs have a nail on each finger rather than a claw, and they handle their food with great delicacy. They usually pull thin branches to their mouth and eat the fruits directly from the tree. If the fruits are very large, however, the lemurs pick them off the tree before eating them.

A hungry ring-tailed lemur takes a delicate bite of fruit from a tamarind tree.

21

Each ring-tailed
lemur must know
its place in the
strict social order
of its group.

Living Together

Ring-tailed lemurs live in groups of between 5 and 30 animals. A typical group consists of six males, eight females, four youngsters, and four babies.

In a group of ring-tailed lemurs, the females are in charge. They decide where the group eats, sleeps, and travels. Females spend their whole life with the group into which they were born. Males, however, might move from one group to another several times in their life.

Status is very important in ring-tailed lemur society. Every group member has its own rank. When scuffles over food or sleeping spots break out, the lower-ranking lemur will always back down. All too often a high-ranking male will chase a lower-ranking one away from a tasty bunch of figs. Usually, though, he will then lose out to one of the females—all of whom have more status than even the highest-ranking male.

A Day in the Life

Although ring-tailed lemurs can see well in the dark, they are usually active only during the day. They wake at sunrise and spend the cool hours of the morning searching for food. Most food is found from 50 to 100 feet (15 to 30 m) above the ground. There, the leafy tops of the trees overlap, forming almost a ceiling of leaves. This layer of thick leaves is known as the forest **canopy**.

At about midday, ring-tailed lemurs take a break from feeding for a few hours. They spend this time dozing in the shade, either on the lower branches of a favorite tree or on the forest floor. It is a quiet time with none of the chasing and squabbling that occurs during feeding. Lemurs love to have close contact with one another. They often huddle together with their feet and tails sticking out in all directions. Midday is also a good time for one of their favorite pastimes—**grooming**.

Ready for a midday snooze, this ring-tailed lemur settles down in the fork of its favorite tree.

Lemurs groom
each other all
over—including
the snout!

Keeping Clean

Lemurs have a coat of thick fur that needs constant attention. Luckily, lemurs love nothing more than spending the hot, sleepy hours of the day combing bugs and matted clumps out of one another's fur.

The tiny gaps between a lemur's bottom teeth form a kind of natural comb. Lemurs also have a long nail on their second toe that is a perfect tool for scratching themselves in a doglike way.

Grooming one another's fur is more than just a practical way of cleaning those hard-to-reach places. It is also an important social activity that helps keep lemur groups close together. When it comes to grooming, rank is not important. The highest-ranking female in the group will happily groom the fur of the lowliest male.

Lemur Voices

In the dense growth of tropical forests, it is often impossible to see farther than the next tree. So the best way for the forest animals to communicate with one another is by making a lot of noise.

Ring-tailed lemurs have a call for every occasion. When searching for food, they will often yelp softly to one another. That stops any members of the group from straying too far away and getting lost. Loud barks serve a different purpose. They alert other lemurs to the presence of humans, birds of prey, and other **predators**.

Just before they go to sleep each night, male ring-tailed lemurs utter a hooting cry that is loud enough to carry for more than ½ mile (1 km). The hooting cry is directed at other groups nearby and is the lemur's way of saying, "Stay away—this is our patch!"

Shouts echo through the forest as a ring-tailed lemur calls to its friends from a tree branch.

On guard duty—a ring-tailed lemur climbs a tree in the spiny desert to keep watch for intruders.

Stay Away!

Ring-tailed lemurs live in a fixed **territory** that they defend against other groups of ring-tailed lemurs. If too many ring-tailed lemurs were to live in one patch of forest, there might not be enough food to go around.

The size of a group's territory depends on the kind of forest in which it lives. In dense forest, where there are plenty of fruiting trees, territories range from about 15 to 20 acres (6 to 8 ha) in size. The lemurs that live in those territories rarely need to walk more than ½ mile (1 km) in the course of a day. In scrubby, open forest, where food is harder to find, territories can be four times as big.

No Trespassers!

Ring-tailed lemurs spend a lot of time patrolling the borders of their territories. By marking these borders with scent, they make sure that neighboring groups have no excuse for trespassing.

Female ring-tailed lemurs produce a smelly liquid from a special gland just below their tail. When a female finds a tree she wants to scent mark, she performs a handstand and rubs her backside against the bark. Males can do that as well, but they prefer to gouge their scent into trees using horny spikes on their wrists.

As the borders of ring-tailed territories often overlap slightly, a group may disagree with the placement of another group's marks. If that happens, all the group members line up beside the offending tree and mark it, one by one, until eventually the smell has been completely changed to their own.

Male lemurs also rub scent into their tail, which they brandish over their head to scare off intruders.

Stink Fights

Neighboring groups of ring-tailed lemurs rarely meet. They smell the scent-marked boundaries of their neighbors' territories and do their best to avoid ever being in the same place at the same time.

However, if one group finds another group in its territory, the females will run at the intruders and begin to fight. The males in both groups tend to stay back, preferring to concentrate on the less risky business of scent-marking.

Male ring-tailed lemurs do have one means of defending their territory, though. If necessary, they can draw their tail between their wrists, covering the tail with scent. Then, by jerking their tail over their head like a catapult, the males are able to propel long-distance stink bombs at their opponents!

Showing Off

Female ring-tailed lemurs can mate for only one day each year in April or May. In the weeks leading up to that day, the males in the group start behaving oddly. For most of the year, low-ranking males will always back down to high-ranking ones. During the mating season, however, rank is forgotten. All the males in the group compete to impress the females.

After some shouting matches and stink-bomb fights the real fighting begins. Males circle one another in a kind of bobbing dance, slashing each other viciously with their teeth.

The stakes are high—the victorious males are allowed to mate and are promoted in rank until the following mating season, when they will be put to the test again. Defeated males might find themselves with a much lower rank than they had previously enjoyed.

A ring-tailed lemur keeps a sharp eye out for danger while her baby dozes on her back.

A baby lemur looks out at the world over its mother's shoulder.

A Seat with a View

Ring-tailed lemurs give birth to a single baby, or occasionally twins, between August and November. That is the beginning of the Madagascan spring—the time when there is the most food in the forest. Since all the babies in a group are born at exactly the same time of year, it is important that there is plenty of food available to feed the extra mouths.

An infant lemur clings to its mother's tummy for the first two weeks of its life, **suckling** on her milk. As soon as the baby is strong enough, it climbs up onto its mother's back for a seat with a view, resting its head between her ears. Infants are very comfortable in this position. They sleep soundly even when their mothers leap from branch to branch!

Growing Up

Ring-tailed lemurs grow up fast. After only three weeks, the youngsters start leaving their mothers to play with one another and work on their climbing skills. At the first sign of danger, however, a young lemur will scamper back to bury its head in its mother's fur.

Infant lemurs are the center of attention in the group. Everyone loves to play with them, and the females will happily allow their babies to be suckled by other mothers. Childless females look after other lemurs' young and sometimes even adopt the second baby when twins are born.

At five months old, ring-tailed lemurs are **weaned** off their mother's milk and start to eat solid foods. From this point on, they must look after themselves. It takes another two and a half years before the young females are old enough to breed. Males develop slightly faster and are usually big and strong enough to win mates two year after weaning.

The young lemur
(left) will soon be
too old to travel
on its mother's back.

A sifaka mother hops across a forest clearing with her baby.

Leaping Lemurs

The largest lemurs are the indris and the sifakas. These monkey-sized creatures are also known as "leaping lemurs." They spend their days in the highest branches of the forest canopy, feeding on fruit, leaves, and buds.

Both of these types have extremely long, powerful back legs, and they can jump across gaps of up to 33 feet (10 m). Since their legs are a third longer than their arms, they cannot walk on all fours. On their rare trips down from the trees they stand upright and move with an unsteady-looking kind of hop-dance, waving their arms in the air for balance.

Indris and sifakas are the noisiest of all the lemurs. The indri's howl is so loud it can carry across more than 2 miles (3 km) of forest.

Night Creatures

Most species of lemurs have large, round eyes that reflect light. That helps the lemurs see in the dark. Even ring-tailed lemurs, sifakas, and indris, which are active by day, share this feature.

For mouse lemurs the ability to see in the dark is essential. These tiny creatures spend their days curled up in a nest made of leaves or in a hollow tree. They emerge only at night. They eat fruit, flowers, insects, and—when they can—eggs and baby birds. Mouse lemurs store fat in their tail to help them through the drier months, when food is scarce in the forest.

Mouse lemurs are good climbers. They can leap distances more than 10 feet (3 m)—quite an achievement considering that they are only 4 to 5 inches (10 to 12 cm) long!

The mouse lemur is active at night. It sleeps through the day in a hidden nest.

Aye ayes are now very rare and may disappear altogether unless steps are taken to protect them.

Aye Aye

The cat-sized aye aye is considered the most peculiar lemur of all. Its huge, batlike ears, grizzled, gray-black coat, and long, thin fingers give it a scary appearance. In Madagascar, seeing an aye aye has long been regarded as a sign of bad luck.

The bulk of the aye aye's diet is made up of grubs and wood-boring insects. Its ears are so sensitive that when it taps on tree trunks to disturb its **prey**, it can hear them scurrying around inside. Once an aye aye has heard some grubs, it bites through the bark and pulls them out with its long third finger.

Aye ayes are also fond of fruit and nuts. As you would expect, hard **husks** are no problem for an animal that can bite through wood!

In the Future

If monkeys had been able to reach the island of Madagascar, the lemurs would have died out long ago. Whether or not they can survive the arrival of the smartest primates of all—humans—is another question altogether.

Between 1,500 and 2,500 years ago, the first people arrived on Madagascar. At this time, the whole island was covered with trees. As the human population grew, more and more trees were chopped down to make way for farmland. Today only one-tenth of the original forest remains, and more trees are destroyed every day. As the forests are cut down, the lemurs lose their homes. Unless people stop clearing the forests, many species of lemurs are certain to disappear.

However, in recent years, **conservation** projects have been set up to protect areas of forest and their lemurs. In addition, some areas of Madagascar are being reforested. **Zoologists** are reintroducing lemurs into these new forests. That offers hope for their survival in the future.

Words to Know

Adapted   Become better suited to.

Canopy   The crowns of the trees, forming a leafy layer of the forest, where many animals live.

Conservation   The protection of animals, plants, and their habitats.

Droughts   Long periods without rain when the land becomes very dry.

Grooming   Cleaning and combing the fur. Lemurs might groom their own fur or that of another lemur in their group.

Habitats   Types of places where animals or plants live.

Husks   The dry outer coverings of some fruits, seeds, and nuts.

Opposable thumb   A thumb that can be moved across the palm to meet the fingers of the same hand.

Predators   Animals that hunt other animals for food.

Prey   An animal hunted by other animals.

Primates	A group of animals that includes humans, apes, monkeys, and lemurs.
Prosimians	The group of primates to which lemurs belong.
Rain forest	A dense tropical forest in an area of high rainfall. Rain forests are extremely rich in plant and animal life.
Simians	Monkeys and apes.
Species	The scientific word for animals of the same type that breed together.
Spiny desert	A dry grassland scattered with cactuslike trees to the west of the mountains in Madagascar.
Suckling	Drinking the mother's milk.
Territory	An area that an animal lives in and defends against intruders of its own kind.
Weaned	When a baby mammal gradually replaces its diet of milk with solid food.
Zoologists	Scientists who study animals.

Find Out More

Books

Dennard, D. *Lemur Landing: A Story of a Madagascan Tropical Dry Forest*. Minneapolis, Minnesota: Tandem Library, 2003.

Martin, P. A. F. *Lemurs, Lorises, and Other Lower Primates*. True Books. Danbury, Connecticut: Children's Press, 2000.

Web sites

Creature Feature: Ring-tailed Lemurs
kids.nationalgeographic.com/Animals/CreatureFeature/Ring-tailed-lemur
Pictures and information about the most well-known type of lemur.

Ring-tailed Lemur
www.enchantedlearning.com/subjects/mammals/primate/Rtlemurprintout.shtml
Facts about the ring-tailed lemur and a diagram to print.

Index